D1545630

Paint & Poetry

An Ekphrastic Journey

Terry Brett & Chip Webster

The Muse

In the 2013 movie *Words and Pictures*, Juliette Binoche (the painter) and Clive Owen (the poet) debate and feud over which of their mediums has more power to influence the world.

It's a clever story with no clear answer. All of us have been moved and inspired by the written word. And a picture, as they say, can tell a thousand stories.

That inspiration is the genesis of our collaboration which began in 2015. A challenge if you will, to dare as well as inspire a fellow artist. We started by using existing pieces we had already created, sending each other five paintings or poems, and having the other interpret them in his artistic medium. This led to an exchange back and forth. Chip would write a new poem, send it to Terry, who would then do his best to interpret the written word, the message, the meaning, the inspiration, and apply paint to canvas. The paintings that followed were quick studies, less than a few minutes each. The feeling of immediacy should be apparent. And then of course, turnabout is fair play. Terry would paint a quick study, and Chip would drill deep to share his inspiration with the pen. Chip is old school. Like many writers, sometimes it flows easily, other times, not so much. He only goes to the computer once the pen and journal have finished their work.

Of course, Chip and Terry did not invent this interchange of interpreting and sharing impressions of another's creation. It has been going on for centuries. As with any wonderful collaboration, theirs started strong, had a couple of bumps and delays, picked up again, and finally resulted in 45 pairs of poems and paintings. You will see most of them in this book. Some are funny, some sad, some in between. We hope you enjoy them all. The challenge for our readers is to figure out who was interpreting whom! See if you can guess which one came first, the poem or the painting. Answers can be found on page 80.

Table of Contents

IN PRAISE OF WOMEN

After all, Ginger Rogers did everything Fred Astaire did.
She just did it backwards and in heels.

Ann Richards

When I reflect on all their talents
Women are the most amazing gender of our species

I am amazed and in awe
What we expect of them and what they deliver over and over

They are the glue that holds our families and communities together
They are most important to survival of our species

Men are different
Loved by our moms
Loved by our partners

Each gender has a different role

We are equal but not the same

Vive La Différence

MOON BEAMS

My moon setting in the west is rising in your east

Know that on your moon beams my love notes travel

Oh my lover knowing that on the same moon we gaze

Brings joy to me each day

THE FIRST KISS

Should I
Shouldn't I
What if she doesn't like me

We are embracing
We are dancing
To a soulful song

It seems right
It seems at last
It is time to kiss
This beautiful woman

I give in and put my lips to hers
And magic happens

It was as though I had never kissed before
There was energy passing between us

I kiss her neck
She melts into my arms
Then a deep kiss
Her tongue meets mine

And it happens

A bolt of energy between us
What was a tentative should I or shouldn't I
Becomes an energy force of us

Not me... not her ... us

MIRROR IN THE STEAM BATH

Letting the moist heat penetrate her body

Penetrating her thoughts

What does she see

Others see a unique beauty

Intellectually brilliant

But what does she see through the fog on the mirror

What she sees is unimportant

What she feels says it all

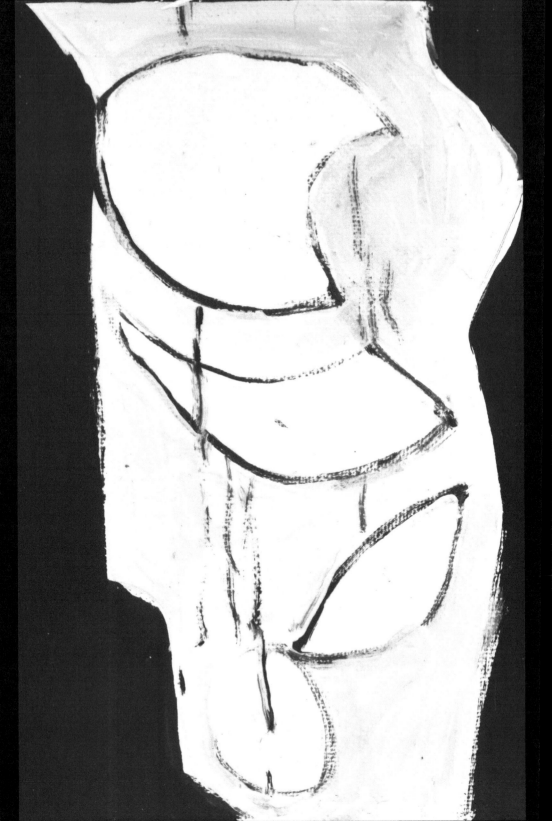

TANGLED UP IN YOU

Laying together in our special space
Detached from the world
I'm tangled up in you

Laying in your arms in our place of passion
Separated from all the world's troubles
I'm tangled up in you

Laying together just focused on you
What's outside doesn't matter
When I'm tangled up in you

CHILDREN

Pink
Sweet
They arrive
Full of wonder
Full of joy

They keep us up at night
Crying
Hungry
Out too late

Will they be happy
Will they find a job
Will they fail

Then they bring us
A pink faced
Grandchild

And
Mankind gets
Another chance

ENDINGS

The chilling sleet scratches at the window
The hazy glow of the streetlight reflects off
the waiting cab's dull yellow paint

The scent of her sweet perfume clings to my body
The memory of her body pressed to mine draws me back to bed
But it has all been said
There is no going back

I dress while watching her fitful sleep
Is she really asleep or wanting to avoid the ending
As I see the curve of her body under the blanket
I remember the passion that brought us together

I tiptoe from her room and from her life
Not wanting to wake her
We'd said it all
Felt it all

As I slid onto the cold vinyl seat and said *LaGuardia* to the driver
I glanced up to the dark window with the pain of loss

What could have been
Got lost in what was

The empty streets of a sleeping New York
reflect the empty feeling in my gut
Another ending

The bright lights of *LaGuardia* bring me back to
the now and a place no longer of endings
But of another beginning

ISLAND IN THE SUN

Sitting on my island

Feeling the sun on my face
Smelling the salt air

My mind runs free
My soul is fed

The crack of the whip
Brings me back to reality

Time to return to the field
And my master

BLACK AND WHITE

It all seems black and white to me

Then I study each element

Each stroke of the brush

Going deeper

It turns to gray

Delving deeper

I see the complexity of it all

It isn't black and white after all

WE CAN'T EXPLAIN IT ALL

We can't explain it all

The angles

The randomness
Of life

We go in one direction
We detect it is wrong

We go in another direction
It feels wrong

All of a sudden
It fits

It makes sense

It just feels right

We can't explain it all

MAYA ANGELOU

Sweet angel of love
You rose above
To show us how to love

Years of silence
Years of abandonment
Years of abuse

You took it all in
You took the hate and turned it to love
You chose to rise above

May the love you left behind
Radiate through all mankind

MOON QUESTIONS

Oh moon floating in
The clear cold sky

What do you know

What questions can I ask you
What questions will you ask me

Why are you there
Why am I here

Are we just floating through the universe together
With no answers

Do you know a secret

Are you waiting
For the right time to tell me

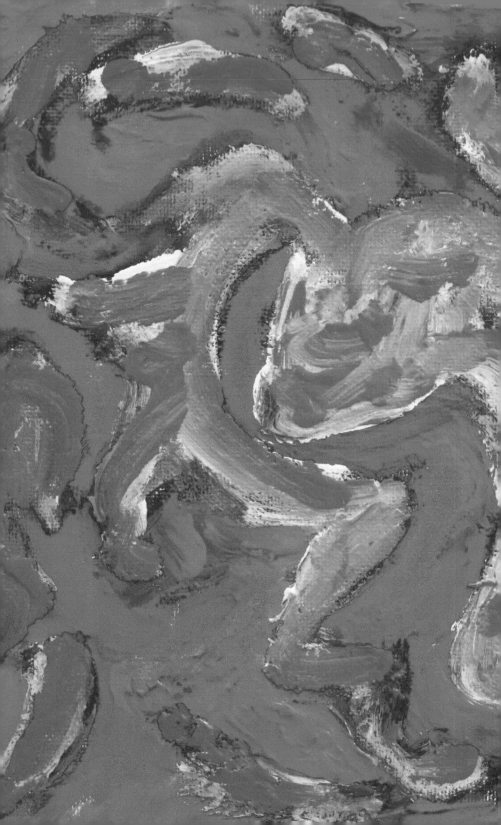

VULNERABILITY

An uncomfortable risk
An unnatural place to be

It frees me to be real
The conversations are richer
The relationships deeper
The friendships more authentic

Life is freer
Unencumbered by all the things I was hiding behind

Now I can grow
By just being who I am
Not burdened by pretense

Life is free

PASSION

Burning deep inside our beings
There is a passion waiting to be tapped

It may be a deeply held political belief

A yet to be discovered cure for cancer

A yet to be developed talent for art

If the passion is never brought to the light of day
It will just smolder

Release the red hot passion of your life
Like a raging fire that brings your gifts to the world

PATCHWORK LIFE

It felt so good to think life was perfect

The whole ride would be smooth

Seamless

But that was self-delusion

It has been a journey of collecting scraps
For my patchwork life

Sewing them together

With bright and dark threads

Joy of winning
Pain of losing

Reaching heights I never dreamed of
Then dreams fading into reality

Passion of love
Pain of loss

Sewn into a patchwork quilt
That keeps me warm in reflection

REFLECTIONS ON A RAINY DAY

The bay turns from blue to gray

Clouds boil up white and puffy
Then darken

The wind makes cats paws on the water

Then the trumpeting thunder
announces the rain

Lightning showing the way

As the raindrops flow
Down my window

My mind drifts away

To the rain on another day

ANGELS

Trying to figure out the universe

Can be tiring

So many variables

So many surprises

So many disappointments

Why are we here

Why the hell are we here

To be angels for each other

Angels in human form

Angels to lift us up when we are down

Angels to open the door to a bigger world

Angels to let us know we are loved

DEVILS TOWER

Monument to the Earth

Standing on the prairie

Reminding us
Beneath our feet
The world is alive

The tower was pushed up
Through Earth's crust

To remind us again
We are on a living planet

TWO DOGS WAITING TO SEE ME

Two dogs waiting to see me

Two dogs waiting to play

Two dogs waiting to be fed

Two dogs just waiting for me

Is there anyone else just waiting for me

AFTERNOON ON MY JET SKI

I got away from the TV
I got away from the iPad
I got away from the cell phone

I cranked up the engine and rode hard
Wanting to get away from the grind
Chasing cormorants
Jumping wakes

I ran out of gas
There was silence

I suddenly saw
Manatees
Dolphin
Turtles

I had never taken time to just stop
And enjoy the silence of the sea
And how it comes alive

I think I'll buy a kayak

DO YOU LIKE WINE

Do you like wine

I do

Usually red
Sometimes white

Sometimes I get a little tight

Would you like some wine tonight

MEETING MYSELF AT MY OWN DOOR

If I run fast enough from myself
If I ignore all my thoughts

I can avoid confronting myself
Dealing with the unfinished business of life

Admitting failures
Mourning loss
Saying I'm sorry

Just keep moving
Watching movies
Buying stuff
Going to games

Then the day comes
A knock on the door
A divorce
A heart attack
The death of a sister I didn't tell "I love you"

I look at the image in the mirror
I'm not 18
I'm 72

I'm tired of running
Stuffing hollow things into the holes of my life

I have a choice
Keep running
Or reflect on and savor all of life's ups and downs

Discover my true essence
The one that has been with me all along

The true essence

Of me

COME TO MY GARDEN

Come sit with me in my garden

Breathe in the sweet smell of flowers

Feel the warm sun on your shoulders

Hear the buzz of bees

Sit with me and absorb

God's love for you and me

OLD TOES

Discolored
Wrinkled
Old people's toes

I used to be repulsed
At the sight when I saw
Old people's toes

Today I looked at my feet
And saw
Old people's toes

Then I remembered
Dancing
Skiing
Running
With my young toes

Now I see
My wise old toes

HOURGLASS

DAMN IT

Who nailed the hour glass to the floor
I want to turn it over and get more time

DAMN IT

Who covered the top chamber so I can't see
how many grains of sand I have left

All I can see is the sand piling up into the bottom chamber

Life already spent

DAMN IT

I want to know how many grains of sand I have left

Then again

Maybe I don't

THE HOUSE OF DARKNESS

Curtains drawn
Sun blocked out
House in disarray
Dirty dishes stacked in the sink
Dust spreading its gray pall

With mixed emotions
We wait for the final gasp of life

Then the curtains will open
The sun will shine in

And the sweet joyful voices
Of grandchildren will bring life back

To the house of darkness

A TERMINAL DIAGNOSIS

March 27, 1946 I was born
March 27, 1946 I was given a terminal diagnosis

I've spent most of my life ignoring reality

The time I spent in denial felt so good
      I'm different
      I'll never die

So deep in denial

The day I was born
Was the first day of my terminal diagnosis

If someone could have made me understand

I would have lived life more fully
      Loved with more passion
      Taken more risks
      Not been afraid to lose

It's not too late

Life is a terminal diagnosis

WINTER MOON

Curled up in my snug bed
Red quilt up to my chin

I look out the window
At the cold winter moon

It seems that on cold clear nights

Memories of you
Come rushing back

CONTACTS

I was scrolling through my contacts

Then his name came up
Then her name came up

A chill ran down my spine

What do I do

What do I do with the contacts of my friends who no longer walk
on this earth
All I would have to do is push the number on the screen
But they won't answer

As much as I'd like to call them
I can't

Someone once said
A person is still alive
As long as someone remembers them

If I delete them from my contacts will I forget them

Will they die again

LESSONS FROM THE
INTERSTATE OF LIFE

On the 405, 5, 95 or 80
I discover my flaws

I'm cruising at 75 in a 65
I run up behind a car cruising at 60 in the left lane and call them an idiot
At 75 I get passed by a car doing 85 – they're crazy

Mile after mile of reflection it dawns on me
Those who disagree with me are either idiots or crazy

Hmm...
So those who vote differently than me – are idiots or crazy?
Those that are different than me are wrong?
So I must be the center of the universe?

Quick - Give me a mirror so I can see this genius
Oh damn
It's me

The guy who missed his exit
The guy who accidentally cut off the car next to him
The guy who voted for an empty suit

One of the many people on the 405 who just wants to get home
To cook dinner
Spend time with his children
Watch the Dodgers

I need to have more empathy

We need to have more empathy

Let the other car into your lane
They just want to get home too

ANOTHER DAMN TO DO LIST

Another damn to do list

I just wrote one and nothing gets done

Ok, maybe one or two
But little else

Now I'm writing another damn to do list with 15 things to do

How far will I get on this one?

WASTED ENERGY

All the energy we spend being right
All the energy we spend making them wrong

The... my team has all the answers
The... your team has never been right

The... we are special and we're going to heaven and you're not... fantasy

Guess what

We are all on the same journey to the end of our lives

Nobody was made by anyone else but God

Your God
My God
One God

We are all headed to the same place
Just on different paths

LIFE PATTERNS

The crazy patterns of life

        The dark times when
        I felt helpless
        My life didn't matter

The bright times
I felt fully alive
My life mattered

        The golden times
        I felt blessed
        My life was balanced

Life isn't always smooth

           That would be boring

NEW MOON

On the dark moonless nights

The ones that are the darkest
Are cold winter nights

The stars fill the sky
As the chill fills my body

I wonder will the full summer moon
Come back again to brighten my nights

The phases of the moon are like phases of life

Yet in its darkest phase
It is called a new moon

AFTER ALL THOSE LONG COLD NIGHTS

After all those long cold nights
After all those gray winter days

The red flower comes again
The green shoots of life sprout up
Through the cold mud of spring

The bush comes to life again
The flower warmed by the sun
Gives us the gift of her beauty

TERRY BRETT

A native of St. Petersburg, FL, Terry comes from a family of artists. His grandmother Ruth Willbrand, was an award-winning artist of distinction, painting figurative and abstract art during the mid-century period. Her daughter and Terry's mother, Gail Willbrand Brett, was an accomplished portrait painter.

Terry studied with Melissa Christiano and Luis de la Lama. His earlier work, focusing on impressionistic urban city scapes, was inspired by Colin Campbell Cooper, Guy Wiggins, and Paul Cornoyer.

Terry's more recent larger, abstract pieces are influenced by Franz Kline, Willem deKooning, and Mark Rothko. His large black and white compositions have the feel of immediacy and power.

Terry held a **One Man Show** at Interior Motives Gallery in 2012. In 2016 his **Blunt Force** show at ARTicles Gallery featured his large black and white compositions. In 2019, his *Iconic Renaissance* show at the Morean Arts Center featured his most recent creations, gold leaf mosaic paintings ranging from the spiritual to the mythic.

He exhibits at Leslie Curran Gallery, ARTicles in St. Petersburg, The Red Herring in Tampa, and Canvas Fashion Gallery in St. Petersburg and Hyde Park, Tampa.

Terry is a past Chairman of the Morean Arts Center, and lives in St. Petersburg.

CHIP WEBSTER

Chip Webster was born in California and currently resides in St. Petersburg, Florida. Chip resisted poetry and writing for most of his life, until he was dragged off the basketball court to hear the poet David Whyte. It was a transformational experience. He has since attended the David Whyte's Invitas - The Foundations of Conversational Leadership course and has been on walking tours with David in Ireland and Italy. In addition, he has been coached by poet and author Dr. Heather Sellers. His first book "A PASSION FOR LIFE, Reflections From The Journey" is available at Amazon.com.

He graduated from Drake University and spent much of his career with Vistage, leading CEO peer forums both as a group Chair and eventually as President of Vistage Florida. He is a past recipient of the Vistage International Don Cope Memorial Award and co-founded TEC/Vistage *Keepers of the Flame*. He has two grown sons and is married to Dr. Debra Doud.

Which Came First

Title	First
In Praise of Women	Painting
Moonbeams	Poem
The First Kiss	Poem
Mirror in the Steam Bath	Painting
Tangled Up in You	Painting
Children	Poem
Endings	Poem
Island in the Sun	Painting
Black and White	Painting
We Can't Explain it All	Poem
Maya Angelou	Poem
Moon Questions	Painting
Vulnerability	Poem
Passion	Painting
Patchwork Life	Painting
Reflections on a Rainy Day	Poem
Angels	Painting
Devils Tower	Poem
Two Dogs Waiting to See Me	Painting
Afternoon on my Jet Ski	Painting
Do You Like Wine?	Poem
Meeting Myself at My Own Door	Poem
Come to My Garden	Painting
Old Toes	Poem
Hourglass	Poem
The House of Darkness	Poem
A Terminal Diagnosis	Poem
Winter Moon	Painting
Contacts	Poem
Lessons From the Interstate of Life	Poem
Another Damn To-Do List	Poem
Wasted Energy	Painting
Life Patterns	Painting
New Moon	Painting
After All Those Long Cold Nights	Painting

Acknowledgments

For Chip one person was paramount in his creative product. Aside from being his best friend, wife, and muse, Dr. Debra Doud encouraged his creativity and helped in the editing process that made his poems more accessible.

For Terry, from the very beginning, his wife Kim has been his biggest fan and supporter. Always encouraging him and challenging him to stretch and take some artistic risk. While she loves all his work, the true compliment comes by making him promise not to sell certain pieces she absolutely loves. Thanks also to Gail and Ruth, Terry's mother and grandmother. While no longer here, both of them passed down the passion for painting and the creative process. Terry would like to thank Darrell Brandimore for his photography.

Saint Petersburg is fortunate to have The Saint Petersburg Press as a resource for artists and writers to have a platform to share their creativity. Thanks to Joe Hamilton for having the vision for the Saint Petersburg Press, to Amy Cianci for keeping us on track to bring our vision into reality, and to Pablo Guidi for his production layout that put it on paper.

Index of First Lines